Amateur Radio Emergency Service®
ARES® Field Resources Manual

A Quick Trainer and Field Resource Guide for the Emergency Communicator

Copyright © 2005-2022
ISBN: 978-0-87259-5439

Published by:

ARRL The National Association for Amateur Radio®

225 Main Street, Newington, CT 06111-1400 USA
www.arrl.org

Foreword

This manual is intended to serve as a quick trainer and reference for amateurs deployed in the field for emergency services work, primarily through the ARRL Amateur Radio Emergency Service (ARES). It provides basic program information, forms and operating aids. A number of templates can be customized for the local area to include reference information such as important phone numbers, emergency frequencies, maps, organizational details and so forth.

Emergency Management Department
Newington, Connecticut
August 2021

ARES® and Amateur Radio Emergency Service® are registered servicemarks of the American Radio Relay League, Incorporated.

Table of Contents

Notes

First Things First

What to Do *First* in Case of an Emergency

1) Check that you and your family are safe and secure before you respond as an ARES volunteer.

2) Check that your property is safe and secure before you respond as an ARES volunteer.

3) Monitor _____ (put your assigned local ARES emergency net frequency here).

4) Follow the instructions you receive from the ARES officials in charge on the above frequency.

5) Contact your local Emergency Coordinator, or his/her designee, for further instructions.

Initial Action Checklist

    The net control station and/or ARES officials on the designated emergency net will provide additional instructions, including information on frequencies used for other resource and tactical nets. Normally, a resource net will enroll volunteers and provide information on how you can assist.

☐ Be prepared to operate. Check all equipment and connections.

☐ Check in with your assigned contact.

☐ Deploy to assignment with "Ready" kit.

☐ Obtain tactical call sign for your location/assignment.

☐ Initiate personal event log (use form at end of this booklet).

☐ Enter assigned frequencies on log sheet and on emergency/frequency plan.

☐ Use log form to record messages handled.

☐ Use a formal message form when a precise record is required.

☐ Use tactical call sign for your location, and observe FCC's 10-minute ID rule.

☐ Monitor your assigned frequency at all times. Notify NCS if you have to leave.

Notes

Equipment and Personal Checklists

Basic Deployment Equipment Checklist

When responding to an emergency event, or even a training exercise, there is a minimum set of equipment and personal gear you should bring with you to get the job done. Basic items include:

☐ 2-meter handheld

☐ 2-meter mag-mount antenna and coax

☐ Earphone

☐ Paper and pencil

☐ ARES ID card

☐ Extra batteries

☐ Appropriate clothing

☐ Food and water

The majority of these items should be kept in a "Ready Kit." Just pick it up on your way out the door for deployment. You might also consider the items on the following list for inclusion in this ready kit, designed to allow you to stay in the field for up to 72 hours.

Extended Deployment (72-Hour) Equipment Checklist

- ☐ Three-day change of clothes
- ☐ Foul weather gear
- ☐ Toilet articles
- ☐ Shelter (tent and sleeping bag)
- ☐ Portable stove;
  (mess kit with cleaning kit)
- ☐ Waterproof matches
- ☐ Flashlight
- ☐ Candles
- ☐ Alarm clock
- ☐ Three-day supply of water and food/snacks

- ☐ Liquid refreshments
- ☐ First aid kit
- ☐ Throat lozenges
- ☐ Prescriptions
- ☐ Aspirin or other pain reliever
- ☐ Additional radios, packet gear
- ☐ Power supplies, chargers
- ☐ Microphones
- ☐ Headphones
- ☐ Patch cords
- ☐ Antennas with mounts
- ☐ SWR bridge (VHF and HF)

- ☐ Extra coax
- ☐ RF connectors and adapters
- ☐ Power, audio and other
  connectors and adapters
- ☐ Batteries
- ☐ Toolbox
- ☐ Soldering iron and solder
- ☐ VOM
- ☐ Electrical and duct tape
- ☐ Safety glasses
- ☐ Log books
- ☐ Message forms

About Your "Ready Kit"

Power—Your 72-hour kit should have several sources of power in it, with extra battery packs and an alkaline battery pack for your handheld. For mobile VHF and UHF radios, larger batteries are needed. Gel-cell or deep-cycle marine batteries are good sources of battery power, and you must keep them charged and ready go. It is also wise to have alternate means available to charge your batteries during the emergency. You can charge smaller batteries from other larger batteries. You can build a solar charging device. If you're lucky, you may have access to a power generator that can be used in place of the normal electrical lines. Have more battery capacity than you think you might need. Have several methods available to connect your radio's different power sources.

Gain Antennas—You can expect to need some kind of gain antenna for your handheld, as well as an additional gain antenna that can be used on either your handheld or your mobile rig. The extra antenna might be needed by someone else, or your first antenna might break. For VHF and UHF, you can build a J-pole from TV twinlead for an inexpensive and very compact antenna. Have several lengths of coax in your kit, totaling at least 50 feet, and barrel connectors to connect them together.

Personal—Include necessities: water, or a reliable water filtration and purification system; enough food for 3 days; eating utensils, a drinking cup and, if needed, a means of cooking your food. Shelter is also important. Here, you are only limited by the size of your kit and your budget. Some hams plan to use their RVs as shelter, conditions permitting. Other disaster conditions may make the use of an RV impossible, so you should have several different plans for shelter. Light is important psychologically during an emergency. Make sure that you have several light sources available. Various battery-powered lights are available, and lanterns that use propane or other fuel are also good possibilities.

Basic Emergency Program Information

Amateur Radio Emergency Service (ARES)

The ARRL Amateur Radio Emergency Service (ARES) consists of licensed amateurs who have voluntarily registered their qualifications and equipment for communications duty in the public interest when disaster strikes. Membership in ARRL or any other local or national organization is not required to join ARES or participate in ARES activities. ARRL membership is, however, required for the leadership appointments described here. Because ARES is an Amateur Radio service, only licensed amateurs are eligible for membership.

ARES Organization

There are three levels of ARES organization—*section*, *district* and *local*. At the section level, the Section Emergency Coordinator (SEC) is appointed by the Section Manager (SM) and works under his supervision. The SM is elected by the ARRL members in the section. In most sections, the SM delegates to the SEC the administration of the section emergency plan and the authority to appoint District Emergency Coordinators (DECs), Assistant District Emergency Coordinators (ADECs) and local Emergency Coordinators (ECs) to help him or her run the ARES program in the section. An Assistant Section Emergency Coordinator may be appointed by either the SM or SEC.

Most of the ARES organization and operation gets accomplished at the local level. The local level is where most emergencies occur. It is also where ARES leaders make direct contact with the ARES member-volunteers and with officials of the agencies to be served. The local EC is therefore the key contact in ARES. The EC is appointed by the SEC, usually on the recommendation of the DEC (if there is one). Depending on how the SEC has set up the section for administrative purposes, the EC may have jurisdiction over a small community or a large city, an entire county or even a group of counties. Whatever jurisdiction is assigned, the EC is in charge of *all* ARES activities in his or her area, not just one interest group, one agency, one club or one band.

In large sections, the SEC has the option of grouping EC jurisdictions into *districts* and appointing a District EC to coordinate the activities of the local ECs. In some cases, the districts may conform to the boundaries of governmental planning or emergency operations districts, while in others they are simply based on repeater coverage or geographical boundaries.

Special-interest groups are headed up by Assistant Emergency Coordinators (AECs). AECs are designated by the EC to supervise activities of groups operating in certain bands, especially those groups that play an important role at the local level, but they may be designated in any manner the EC deems appropriate. These assistants, with the EC as chairman, constitute the local ARES "planning committee," which meets to discuss problems and plan projects to keep the ARES group active and well trained.

There are any number of different situations and circumstances that might confront an EC, and the EC's ARES unit should be organized in anticipation of them. There is no specific point at which organization ceases and operation commences. Both phases must be concurrent because a living organization is a changing one, and the operations must change with the organization.

National Traffic System (NTS)

The National Traffic System (NTS) is designed to meet two principal objectives: 1) Rapid movement of traffic from origin to destination, and 2) training amateur operators to handle written traffic and participate in directed nets. NTS operates daily and consists of four different net levels—area, region, section, and local. The four levels operate in an orderly sequence to make a definite flow pattern for traffic, from origin to destination.

Local Nets

Local nets are those covering small areas such as a community, city, county or metropolitan area, not a complete ARRL section. They usually operate at VHF (typically 2-meter FM) at times and on days most convenient to their members. Some are designated as emergency (ARES) nets that do not specialize in traffic handling. Local nets are intended mainly for local delivery of traffic. Some NTS local nets operate daily, just like other nets of the system, to provide outlets for locally originated traffic. They also route the incoming traffic as closely as possible to its actual destination before delivery—a matter of practice in a procedure that might be required in an emergency. Most local nets, and even some section nets in smaller sections, are using repeaters to excellent effect. Average coverage on VHF can be extended using a strategically located repeater, and this can achieve a local coverage area wide enough to encompass many of the smaller sections.

Section Nets

Coverage of the section may be accomplished by individual stations reporting in, by representatives of NTS local nets, or both. The section may have more than one net (a CW net, a VHF net and an SSB net, for example). Section nets are administered by an appointed Section Traffic Manager (STM) or designated Net Managers (NMs). The purpose of the section net is to handle traffic within the section and distribute traffic coming to the section from higher NTS levels. The section net also puts traffic bound for destinations outside the section in the hands of the person who is designated to report into the next-higher NTS level (the region level). A high level of participation by amateurs within the section is desirable to carry out all of these responsibilities.

Operation During Disasters

When a disaster situation arises, NTS is capable of expanding its cyclic operation into complete or partial operations as needed. ECs in disaster areas determine the communications needs and make decisions regarding the disposition of local communications facilities, in coordination with agencies to be served. The SEC, after conferring with the affected DECs and ECs, makes recommendations to the Section Traffic Manager and/or NTS net managers at section and/or region levels. The decision and resulting action to alert the NTS region management may be performed by any combination of these officials, depending upon the urgency of the situation. While the EC is, in effect, the manager of ARES nets operating at local levels, and therefore makes decisions regarding their activation, managers of NTS nets at local, section, region and area levels are directly responsible for activation of their nets in a disaster situation. They activate their nets at the behest of, and on the recommendation of, ARES or NTS officials at lower levels.

Types of Emergency Nets

Tactical Net—The tactical net is the front-line net employed during an incident, usually used by a single government agency to coordinate with amateur radio operations within their jurisdiction. There may be several tactical nets in operation for a single incident, depending on the volume of traffic and number of agencies involved. Communications include traffic handling and resource recruiting.

Resource Net—For larger-scale incidents, a resource net is used to recruit operators and equipment in support of operations on the tactical nets. As an incident requires more operators or equipment, the resource net evolves as a check-in place for volunteers to register and receive assignments.

Command Net—As the size of an incident increases and more jurisdictions become involved in the incident, a command net may become necessary. This net allows the incident managers to communicate with each other to resolve inter- or intra-agency problems, particularly between cities or within larger jurisdictional areas. It is conceivable that this net could become cluttered with a high volume of traffic. It may also be necessary to create multiple command nets to promote efficiency.

Open and Closed Nets—A net may operate as an open or "free form" net, or as a closed net where a net control station (NCS) is used to control the flow of transmissions on the channel. Typically, when the amount of traffic is low or sporadic, a net control isn't required and an open net is used. Stations merely listen before they transmit. When a net is declared a closed net, then *all* transmissions must be directed by the NCS.

Radio Amateur Civil Emergency Service (RACES)

RACES is a part of the Amateur Radio Service that provides radio communications for civil-preparedness purposes only, during periods of local, regional or national civil emergencies. These emergencies are not limited to war-related activities, but can include natural disasters such as fires, floods and earthquakes. RACES is administered by local/county/state emergency management agencies, with guidance from the Federal Emergency Management Agency (FEMA).

Operating Procedure

Amateurs operating in the local RACES must be officially enrolled in the local civil preparedness group. RACES operation is conducted by amateurs using their own primary station licenses and by existing RACES stations. The FCC no longer issues new RACES ("WC" prefix) station call signs. Operator privileges in RACES are dependent upon, and identical to, those for the class of license held in the Amateur Radio Service. All of the authorized frequencies and emissions allocated to the Amateur Radio Service are also available to RACES on a shared basis.

Although RACES was originally based on potential use in wartime, it has evolved over the years. This is also true of the meaning of civil defence — also called civil preparedness or other emergency management — which now encompasses all types of emergencies.

While operating in a RACES capacity, RACES stations and amateurs registered in the local RACES organization may not communicate with amateurs who are not operating in a RACES capacity. Such restrictions do not apply when RACES stations are operating in a non-RACES — such as ARES — amateur capacity. Only civil preparedness/emergency management communications can be transmitted, as defined in the FCC Rules. Tests and drills are permitted for a maximum of 1 hour per week. All test and drill messages must be clearly identified as such.

ARES and RACES

Although ARES and RACES are separate entities, ARRL advocates dual membership and cooperative efforts between both services whenever possible. An ARES group whose members are all enrolled in and certified by RACES may operate in an emergency with great flexibility. Using the same operators and the same frequencies, an ARES group also enrolled as RACES can "switch hats" from ARES to RACES and RACES to ARES to meet the requirements of the situation as it develops. For example, during a "nondeclared emergency," ARES can operate under ARES, but when an emergency or disaster is officially declared by government emergency management authority, the operation can become RACES with no change in personnel or frequencies.

Incident Command System (ICS)

The Incident Command System (ICS) is a managemenat tool being adopted by professional emergency responders throughout the country. ICS provides a coordinated system of command, communications, organization, and accountability in managing emergency events. Amateur radio operators should be familiar with the system, as well as how they will interface with agencies employing the ICS.

Integral to the ICS is the concept of Unified Command. There is only one boss, the Incident Commander, who is responsible for the overall operation. For any incident, a number of functions must be performed, ranging from planning and logistics to handling the press. The functional requirements of planning, logistics, operations, and finance are always present, despite the size of the incident. They may be handled by a single individual for a small incident, or a "Command Staff" for a large incident. Another characteristic of ICS is "span of control." In simple terms, any manager should only directly manage a small number of people -- ICS uses the number five for organizational purposes. That number is a useful organizational guideline, rather than a hard and fast rule.

How does the amateur radio volunteer fit into the Incident Command System? We are expected to be communicators, and within the ICS, this would place us in the Logistics Section of the Service Branch as part of the Communications Unit. The Communications Unit provides all communications services for the operation. A training course, "IS-200.c—Basic Incident Command System," is available as part of the FEMA Independent Study Program at **https://training.fema.gov/is/crslist.aspx**.

National Incident Management System (NIMS)

The National Incident Management System (NIMS) has been developed to help emergency managers and responders from different jurisdictions work together more effectively during emergencies and disasters. The NIMS provides a set of standardized organizational structures, such as the Incident Command System, and standardized processes and procedures. More information about NIMS is available from the FEMA website. See "IS-700.b—National Incident Management System (NIMS), An Introduction," found at **https://training.fema.gov/is/crslist.aspx**.

Notes

Hazardous Material Incident Deployments

HAZMAT Incidents

The term "hazardous materials" (HAZMAT) refers to any substances or materials which, if released in an uncontrolled manner (spilled, for example), can be harmful to people, animals, crops, water systems or other elements of the environment. The list is long and includes explosives, gases, flammable and combustible liquids, flammable solids or substances, oxidizing substances, poisonous and infectious substances, radioactive materials and corrosives.

One of the major problems is to determine what chemicals are where and in what quantities. Various organizations in the US have established or defined classes or lists of hazardous materials for regulatory purposes or for the purpose of providing rapid indication of the hazards associated with individual substances. As the primary regulatory agency concerned with the safe transportation of such materials in interstate commerce, the US Department of Transportation (DOT) has established definitions of various classes of hazardous materials, established placarding and marking requirements for containers and packages, and adopted an international cargo commodity numbering system.

The DOT requires that all freight containers, trucks and rail cars transporting these materials display placards identifying the hazard class or classes of the materials they are carrying. The placards are diamond-shaped, 10 inches on a side, color-coded and show an icon or graphic symbol depicting the hazard class. They are displayed on the ends and sides of transport vehicles. A four-digit identification number may be displayed on the placard or on an adjacent rectangular orange panel.

You have undoubtedly seen these placards or panels displayed on trucks and railroad tank cars. You may recognize some of the more common ones, such as "1993," which covers a multitude of chemicals including road tar, cosmetics, diesel fuel and home heating oil. Or you may have seen tankers placarded "1203" filling the underground tanks at local gasoline stations.

In addition to the placards, warning labels must be displayed on most packages containing hazardous materials. The labels are smaller versions of the placards, at 4 inches on a side. In some cases, more than one label must be displayed, in which case the labels must be placed next to each other. In addition to the labels for each of the DOT hazard classes, other labels with specific warning messages may be required. Individual containers also have to be accompanied by shipping papers, if possible, which contain the proper shipping name, the four-digit ID number and other important information about the hazards of the material.

Details of the placards and emergency response procedures can be found in the comprehensive DOT *Emergency Response Guidebook*, copies of which may be available for review from local civil preparedness officials or your police, sheriff or fire department. You may also want to consult your Local Emergency Planning Committee (LEPC) or State Emergency Response Commission (SERC) concerning what role Amateur Radio might have in your local plan. For more information about hazardous materials in general, contact FEMA, Technological Hazards Division, 500 C St. SW, Washington, DC 20472, or visit **https://www.fema.gov/technological-hazards-division-contacts**. More information is also available from the Pipeline and Hazardous Materials Safety Administration (PHMSA), Office of Hazardous Materials Safety, online at **https://www.phmsa.dot.gov/**.

HAZMAT Incident Guidelines

Approach the scene cautiously—from uphill and upwind. If you have binoculars, use them!

Try to identify the material by any *one* of the following:

- The four-digit number on a placard or orange panel.
- The four-digit number (preceded by the initials "UN/NA") on a shipping paper or package.
- The name of the material on the shipping paper, placard or package.

Call for help *immediately* and let the experts handle the situation. *Do not attempt* to take any action beyond your level of training.

Notes

Basic Operating Principles

Principles of Repeater Operation

1. Use minimum power. Otherwise, especially in heavily populated areas, you run the risk of keying more than one repeater, thus causing unnecessary interference. Low power also conserves batteries.

2. Use simplex, whenever possible. ARRL recommends 146.52 MHz, but it's a good idea to have at least one other simplex channel available. Use a gain antenna at fixed locations for simplex operation.

3. Observe the "pause" procedure between exchanges. When it is your turn to transmit, after the transmitting station stands by, count to two or three before pressing your transmit switch. This gives others with urgent traffic a chance to check in.

4. Listen much, transmit little. Announce your presence on a repeater when you are certain of being able to assist in an emergency, and don't tie it up with idle chatter.

5. Monitor your local ARES net frequency when you are not otherwise busy.

6. Think before you talk. Stick to facts, control your emotions. Remember, during an emergency is the time when you are most apt to act and speak rashly. Anyone with an inexpensive public service band receiver can monitor.

7. Articulate, don't slur. Speak close to your mic, but talk across it, not into it. Keep your voice down. In an emergency situation, you may get excited and tend to shout. Talk slowly, calmly — this is the mark of an experienced communicator.

Principles of Disaster Communication

1. Keep transmissions to a minimum. In a disaster, crucial stations may be weak. All other stations should remain silent unless they are called upon. If you're not sure you should transmit, don't.

2. Monitor established disaster frequencies. Many ARES localities and some geographical areas have established disaster frequencies where someone is always (or nearly always) monitoring for possible calls.

3. Avoid spreading rumors. During and after a disaster situation, especially on the phone bands, you may hear almost anything. Unfortunately, much misinformation is transmitted. Rumors are started by expansion, deletion, amplification or modification of words, and by exaggeration or interpretation. All addressed transmissions should be officially authenticated as to their source. These transmissions should be repeated word for word, if at all, and only when specifically authorized.

4. Authenticate all messages. Every message that purports to be of an official nature should be written and signed. Whenever possible, amateurs should avoid initiating disaster or emergency traffic themselves. We do the *communicating*; the agency officials we serve supply the *content* of the communications.

5. Strive for efficiency. Whatever happens in an emergency, you will find hysteria and some amateurs who are activated by the thought that they must be sleepless heroes. Instead of operating your own station full time at the expense of your health and efficiency, it is much better to serve a shift at one of the best-located and best-equipped stations, suitable for the work at hand, manned by relief shifts of the best-qualified operators. This reduces interference and secures well-operated stations.

6. Select the mode and band to suit the need. Many amateurs believe that their favorite mode and band is superior to all others. The merits of a particular band or mode in a communications emergency should be evaluated impartially, with a view to the appropriate use of bands and modes. There is, of course, no alternative to using what happens to be available, but there are ways to optimize available resources.

7. Use all communications channels intelligently. While the primary objective of emergency communications is to save lives and property (anything else is incidental), amateur radio is a secondary communications means. Normal channels are primary and should be used if available. Amateurs should be willing and able to use any appropriate emergency channels — amateur radio or otherwise — in the interest of getting the message through.

8. Don't "broadcast." Some stations in an emergency situation have a tendency to emulate "broadcast" techniques. While it is true that the general public may be listening, our transmissions are not — and should not be — made for that purpose.

9. NTS and ARES leadership coordination. Within the disaster area itself, the ARES is primarily responsible for emergency communications support. The first priority of those NTS operators who live in or near the disaster area is to make their expertise available to their Emergency Coordinator (EC) where and when needed. For timely and effective response, this means that NTS operators should talk to their ECs before the time of need so that they will know how to best respond.

Message Formats

Disaster Welfare Message Form

Number	Precedence	HX	Station of Origin	Check	Place of Origin	Time Filed	Date

TO:

Message Receipt or Delivery Information

Operator and station: _____

Sent to: _____

Delivered to: _____

Telephone number:

Date: _____ Time: _____

(Circle no more than two standard texts from list below)

ARL ONE   **Everyone safe here. Please don't worry.**

ARL TWO   **Coming home as soon as possible.**

ARL THREE   **Am in _____ hospital. Receiving excellent care and recovering fine.**

ARL FOUR   **Only slight property damage here. Do not be concerned about disaster reports.**

ARL FIVE   **Am moving to new location. Send no further mail or communications. Will inform you of new address when relocated.**

ARL SIX   **Will contact you as soon as possible.**

ARL SIXTY FOUR   **Arrived safely at _____**

Time	Date	Telephone	Signature	Name

ARRL Message Form Instructions

Every formal radiogram message originated and handled should contain the following four main components in the order given. The numbers and letters refer to corresponding information on the example message on the next page.

1. Preamble

The Preamble includes information used to prioritize and track the message and ensure its accuracy.

(A) Number. Assigned by the Station of Origin and never changed. Begin with 1 each month or year.

(B) Precedence. Determines the order in which traffic is passed. Assign each message a Precedence of R (Routine), W (Welfare), P (Priority) or EMERGENCY. See the guidelines on page 37 of this manual.

(C) Handling Instructions (HX). Optional, used only if a specific need is present. Handling Instructions are detailed on page 39 of this manual.

(D) Station of Origin. The call sign of the station originating (creating) the message.

(E) Check. The number of words or word groups in the text of the message. A word group is any group of one or more consecutive characters with no interrupting spaces.

(F) Place of Origin. The location (city and state) of the party for whom the message was created, and not necessarily the location of the Station of Origin.

(G) Time Filed. Optional, used only when the filing time has some importance relative to the Precedence, Handling Instructions, or Text.

(H) Date. The date the message was filed. If Time Filed is used, date and time must agree.

2. Address

Name, address, city, state, ZIP, and telephone number of the intended recipient, should be as complete as possible. Note that punctuation is not used in the Address section.

3. Text

Message information should be limited to 25 words or fewer, if possible. Normal punctuation characters are not used in the text. A question mark is sent as QUERY, while DASH is sent for a hyphen. The letter x is used as a period — but never after the last group of the text — and counts as a word when figuring the Check. The letter R is used in place of a decimal in mixed figure groups (example: 146R52 for 146.52).

4. Signature

The name of the party for whom the message was originated. May include additional information, such as amateur radio call sign, title, address, phone number, and so on.

<u>**Message Example**</u>

1. Preamble	1	R	HXG	W1AW	8	NEWINGTON CT	1830Z	JULY 1
	(A)	(B)	(C)	(D)	(E)	(F)	(G)	(H)

2. Address   DONALD SMITH
164 EAST SIXTH AVE
NORTH RIVER CITY MO 00789
555 1234

3. Text   HAPPY BIRTHDAY X SEE YOU SOON X LOVE

4. Signature   DIANA

ARRL MESSAGE PRECEDENCES

EMERGENCY—Any involving life and death urgency to any person or group of persons, that is to be transmitted by amateur radio in the absence of regular commercial facilities. This includes official messages of welfare agencies during emergencies requesting supplies, materials, or instructions vital to relief efforts for the stricken populace in emergency areas. On CW and digital modes, this designation will always be spelled out. *When in doubt, do not use this designation.*

PRIORITY—Abbreviated as P on CW and digital modes. This classification is for important messages having a specific time limit, official messages not covered in the emergency category, press dispatches, and emergency-related traffic not of the utmost urgency.

WELFARE—Abbreviated as W on CW and digital modes. This classification refers to an inquiry about the health and welfare of an individual in the disaster area, or to an advisory from the disaster area that indicates all is well. Welfare traffic is handled only after all Emergency and Priority traffic is cleared. The Red Cross equivalent to an incoming Welfare message is DWI (Disaster Welfare Inquiry).

ROUTINE—Abbreviated as R on CW and digital modes. Most traffic in normal times will bear this designation. In disaster situations, traffic labeled Routine should be handled last, or not at all when circuits are busy with higher-precedence traffic.

ARRL — The National Association for Amateur Radio®

NUMBER	PRECEDENCE	HX	STATION OF ORIGIN	CHECK	PLACE OF ORIGIN	TIME FILED	DATE

TO

PHONE NUMBER

Email

THIS RADIO MESSAGE WAS RECEIVED AT

AMATEUR STATION _____ PHONE _____

NAME _____ EMAIL _____

STREET _____

CITY, STATE, ZIP _____

_____ _____ _____ _____ _____

_____ _____ _____ _____ _____

_____ _____ _____ _____ _____

_____ _____ _____ _____ _____

_____ _____ _____ _____ _____

FROM	DATE	TIME	TO	DATE	TIME
REC'D			**SENT**		

This message was handled at no charge by a licensed amateur radio operator, whose address is shown in the box at right above. No compensation can be accepted by a "ham" operator. A return message may be filed with the ham delivering this message to you. Further information on amateur radio may be obtained from ARRL Headquarters, 225 Main Street, Newington, CT 06111 or www.arrl.org.

ARRL is the national association for Amateur Radio. One of its functions is promotion of public service communication among amateur radio operators. To that end, ARRL has organized the National Traffic System for daily nationwide message handling.

01/21

ARRL Message Handling Instructions

Handling instructions (HX) convey special instructions to operators handling and delivering the message. The instruction is inserted in the message Preamble between the Precedence and the Station of Origin. Its use is optional with the originating stations, but once inserted, it is mandatory with all relaying stations.

PROSIGN	INSTRUCTION
HXA	(Followed by number.) Collect landline delivery authorized by addressee within _____ miles. (If no number, authorization is unlimited.)
HXB	(Followed by number.) Cancel message if not delivered within ____ hours of filing time; service originating station.
HXC	Report date and time of delivery (TOD) to originating station.
HXD	Report to originating station the identity of station from which received, plus date and time. Report identity of station to which relayed, plus date and time, or if delivered report date, time and method of delivery.
HXE	Delivering station gets reply from addressee, originates message back.
HXF	(Followed by number.) Hold delivery until _____ (date).
HXG	Delivery by mail or landline toll call not required. If toll or other expense involved, cancel message and service originating station.

ARRL Numbered Radiograms for Possible "Relief Emergency Use"

Numbered radiograms are an efficient way to convey common messages. The letters "ARL" are inserted in the Preamble, in the Check, and in the text before spelled-out numbers that represent texts from this list. Note that some ARL texts include insertion of information.

Example: NR 1 W W1AW ARL 4 NEWINGTON CT DEC 25 DONALD R SMITH 164 EAST SIXTH AVE NORTH RIVER CITY MO PHONE 733 3968 $\overline{BT}$ ARL ONE ARL TWO $\overline{BT}$ DIANA $\overline{AR}$.

ONE   Everyone safe here. Please don't worry.

TWO   Coming home as soon as possible.

THREE   Am in _____ hospital. Receiving excellent care and recovering fine.

FOUR   Only slight property damage here. Do not be concerned about disaster reports.

FIVE   Am moving to new location. Send no further mail or communication. Will inform you of new address when relocated.

SIX   Will contact you as soon as possible.

SEVEN	Please reply by amateur radio through the amateur delivering this message. This is a free public service.
EIGHT	Need additional _____ mobile or portable equipment for immediate emergency use.
NINE	Additional _____ radio operators needed to assist with emergency at this location.
TEN	Please contact _____. Advise to standby and provide further emergency information, instructions, or assistance.
ELEVEN	Establish amateur radio emergency communications with _____ on _____ MHz.
TWELVE	Anxious to hear from you. No word in some time. Please contact me as soon as possible.
THIRTEEN	Medical emergency situation exists here.
FOURTEEN	Situation here becoming critical. Losses and damage from ____ increasing.
FIFTEEN	Please advise your condition and what help is needed.
SIXTEEN	Property damage very severe in this area.
SEVENTEEN	REACT communications services also available. Establish REACT communication with _____ on channel _____.

EIGHTEEN	Please contact me as soon as possible at _____.
NINETEEN	Request health and welfare report on _____(name, address, phone).
TWENTY	Temporarily stranded. Will need some assistance. Please contact me at _____.
TWENTY ONE	Search and Rescue assistance is needed by local authorities here. Advise availability.
TWENTY TWO	Need accurate information on the extent and type of conditions now existing at your location. Please furnish this information and reply without delay.
TWENTY THREE	Report at once the accessibility and best way to reach your location.
TWENTY FOUR	Evacuation of residents from this area urgently needed. Advise plans for help.
TWENTY FIVE	Furnish as soon as possible the weather conditions at your location.
TWENTY SIX	Help and care for evacuation of sick and injured from this location needed at once.

Local Net/Contact Information

Local Emergency Net Information

Date	Time	Net Name	Frequency	Sponsor
		ARES Net		
		RACES Net		
		SKYWARN Net		
		NTS Section Net		
		NTS Local Net		

Local American Red Cross Chapter Offices

Chapter Name	Address	Telephone	Email	Station Call Sign

Local/County Emergency Operations Centers

EOC Name	Address	Telephone	Email	Station Call Sign

Local/County Public Safety Agency Offices

Agency/Office Name	Address	Telephone	Email	Station Call Sign
State Police				
Local Police				
Sheriff				
Fire Department				
Ambulance				
Civil Defense/Emergency Management				
National Weather Service				

Section/District/County ARRL ARES Emergency Coordinators

Name and Call Sign	Title	Address	Telephone	Email
	Emergency Coordinator (EC)			
	Assistant EC			
	Assistant District EC			
	District EC			
	Assistant Section EC			
	Section EC			
	Section Manager			
	Net Manager			

Other Emergency Information Contacts

Name and Call Sign	Title	Address	Telephone	Email

Local Repeater Directory

Location	Output	Input	Call Sign	Notes
				Emergency Power
				Emergency Power

Local Repeater Directory (cont.)

Location	Output	Input	Call Sign	Notes
				Emergency Power
				Emergency Power

ARRL Section ARES Map

Paste your ARRL Section ARES map here. The map may show the breakdown of your ARRL Section into districts and local jurisdictions, or other organizational information.

Section Emergency Plan

Paste your Section Emergency Operations Plan here.

Local Packet Directory

Location	Frequency	Alias	Call Sign	Notes
				Emergency Power
				Emergency Power

Local Packet Directory (cont.)

Location	Frequency	Alias	Call Sign	Notes
				Emergency Power
				Emergency Power

Notes

Operating Aids

Simple Packet BBS Commands

Abbreviation	Command	Function
B	BYE	Disconnect from the mailbox
CM	Copy Msg	Make a copy of a message for another station
D	Download	Download files (Read files that are in the BBS)
E	Edit TFC	Edit the message header (To, From, etc.)
H	Help	Gives a list of BBS commands
J	WHO	Listing of stations recently heard or connected to the mailbox
K	Kill	Kill (erase) a message
L	List	List messages (several variations available)
N	Name	Enter your Name, QTH, Zip, and Home Mailbox
R	Read	Read a message
S	Send	Send a message
U	Upload	Upload a file to the BBS
W	What	What files are on the BBS?

ARRL Communications Procedures

Voice	CW	Function
Go ahead	K	Used after calling CQ, or at the end of a transmission, to indicate any station is invited to transmit.
Over	AR	Used after a call to a specific station, to indicate end of instant transmission.
	KN	Used at the end of any transmission when only the specific station contacted is invited to answer.
Stand by or wait	AS	A temporary interruption of the contact.
Roger	R	Indicates a transmission has been received correctly.
Clear	SK	End of contact. SK is sent before final identification.
Leaving the air	CL	Indicates that a station is going off the air, and will not listen for any further calls. CL is sent after the final identification.

ITU Phonetic Alphabet

Word list adopted by the International Telecommunication Union.

A	ALPHA	J	JULIET	S	SIERRA
B	BRAVO	K	KILO	T	TANGO
C	CHARLIE	L	LIMA	U	UNIFORM
D	DELTA	M	MIKE	V	VICTOR
E	ECHO	N	NOVEMBER	W	WHISKEY
F	FOXTROT	O	OSCAR	X	X-RAY
G	GOLF	P	PAPA	Y	YANKEE
H	HOTEL	Q	QUEBEC	Z	ZULU
I	INDIA	R	ROMEO		

R-S-T System

Readability

1—Unreadable

2—Barely readable, occasional words distinguishable.

3—Readable with considerable difficulty.

4—Readable with practically no difficulty.

5—Perfectly readable.

Signal Strength

1—Faint signals, barely perceptible.

2—Very weak signals.

3—Weak signals.

4—Fair signals.

5—Fairly good signals.

6—Good signals.

7—Moderately strong signals.

8—Strong signals.

9—Extremely strong signals.

Tone

1—Sixty Hz ac or less, very rough and broad.

2—Very rough ac, very harsh and broad.

3—Rough ac tone, rectified but not filtered.

4—Rough note, some trace of filtering.

5—Filtered rectified ac but strongly ripple-modulated.

6—Filtered tone, definite trace of ripple modulation.

7—Near pure tone, trace of ripple modulation.

8—Near perfect tone, slight trace of modulation.

9—Perfect tone, no trace of ripple or modulation of any kind.

International Q Signals

Signal	Message	Signal	Message
QRA	What is the name of your station?	QRQ	Shall I send faster?
QRG	What's my exact frequency?	QRS	Shall I send slower?
QRH	Does my frequency vary?	QRT	Shall I stop sending?
QRI	How is my tone? (1-3)	QRU	Have you anything for me? (Answer in negative)
QRK	What is my signal intelligibility? (1-5)	QRV	Are you ready?
QRL	Are you busy?	QRW	Shall I tell .... you're calling him?
QRM	Is my transmission being interfered with?	QRX	When will you call again?
QRN	Are you troubled by static?	QRZ	Who is calling me?
QRO	Shall I increase transmitter power?	QSA	What is my signal strength? (1-5)
QRP	Shall I decrease transmitter power?	QSB	Are my signals fading?
		QSD	Is my keying defective?

Signal	Message	Signal	Message
QSG	Shall I send .... messages at a time?	QTA	Shall I cancel number .... ?
QSK	Can you work break-in?	QTB	Do you agree with my word count? (Answer negative)
QSL	Can you acknowledge receipt?	QTC	How many messages have you to send?
QSM	Shall I repeat the last message sent?	QTH	What is your location?
QSO	Can you communicate with .... direct?	QTR	What is your time?
QSP	Will you relay to .... ?	QTV	Shall I stand guard for you ..... ?
QSV	Shall I send a series of V's?	QTX	Will you keep your station open for further communication with me?
QSW	Will you transmit on .... ?	QUA	Have you news of .... ?
QSX	Will you listen for .... on .... ?		
QSY	Shall I change frequency?		
QSZ	Shall I send each word/group more than once? (Answer send twice or .....)		

Abbreviations, Prosigns, Prowords

CW	Phone
$\overline{AA}$	(Separation between parts of address or signature.)
AA	All after (use to get fills).
AB	All before (used to get fills).
ADEE	Addressee (name of person to whom message addressed).
ADR	Address (second part of message).
$\overline{AR}$	End of message (end of record copy).
ARL	(Used with "check " indicates use of ARRL numbered message in text).
$\overline{AS}$	Stand by; wait.
B	More (another message to follow).
BK	Break; break me; break-in (interrupt transmission on CW. Quick check on phone).
$\overline{BT}$	Separation (break) between address and text; between text and signature.
C	Correct; yes.
CFM	Confirm. (Check me on this).
CK	Check.
DE	From; this is (preceding identification).
$\overline{HH}$	(Error in sending. Transmission continues with last word correctly sent.)
HX	(Handling instructions. Optional part preamble.) Initial(s). Single letter(s) follow.
$\overline{IMI}$	Repeat; I say again. (Difficult or unusual words or groups.)
K	Go ahead; over; reply expected. (Invitation to transmit .)
N	Negative; incorrect; no more. (No more messages to follow.)
NR	Number. (Message follows.)
PBL	Preamble (first part of message)....... Read back. (Repeat as received.)
R	Roger; point. (Received; decimal point.)
$\overline{SIG}$	Signed; signature (last part of message.)
$\overline{SK}$	Out; clear (end of communications reply expected.)
TU	Thank you.
WA	Word after (used to get fills.)
WB	Word before (used to get fills.) ...... Speak slower. ...... Speak faster.

Hurricane Information

Saffir-Simpson Hurricane Scale

The Saffir-Simpson Hurricane Scale is a 1-5 rating based on a hurricane's intensity. It is used to give an estimate of the potential property damage and flooding expected along the coast from a hurricane landfall. For more information about this scale and hurricanes in general, visit the National Hurricane Center's website at **www.nhc.noaa.gov**.

Cateory	Pressure (inches)	Winds (MPH)	Surge (feet)	Damage
1	28.94	74-95	4-5	No real damage to buildings. Damage to unanchored mobile homes, shrubs, and trees. Some damage to poorly built signs. Some coastal flooding and minor pier damage.
2	28.50	96-110	6-8	Some damage to building roofs, doors, and windows. Considerable damage to shrubs and trees with some trees blown down. Considerable damage to mobile homes, poorly built signs, and piers. Small craft in unprotected anchorages may break moorings.
3	27.91	111-130	9-12	Some structural damage to small residences and utility buildings. Large trees blown down. Mobile homes and poorly built signs destroyed. Flooding near the coast destroyed smaller structures with larger structures damaged by floating debris. Terrain may be flooded well inland. Evacuation of low areas within several blocks of shoreline may be required.
4	27.17	131-155	13-18	More extensive curtainwall failures with some complete roof structure failure on small residences. Shrubs, trees, and all signs blown down. Major erosion of beach areas. Terrain may be flooded well inland. Massive evacuation of low areas up to 6 miles inland may be required.
5	27.16	156+	18+	Complete failure of roofs on residences and many commercial buildings. Some complete building failures with small buildings overturned or blown away. All shrubs, trees, and signs blown down. Flooding caused major damage to all structures near the shoreline. Massive evacuation from low ground within 5-10 miles of the shoreline may be required.

Hurricane Tracking Chart

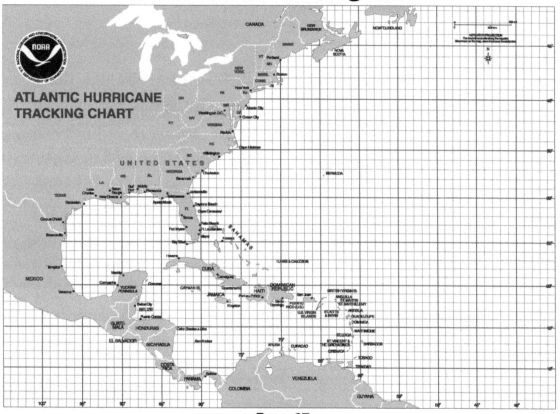

Appendices

Appendix 1

FCC Rules, Subpart E — Providing Emergency Communications

§97.401 Operation during a disaster.

(a) When normal communication systems are overloaded, damaged or disrupted because a disaster has occurred, or is likely to occur, in an area where the amateur service is regulated by the FCC, an amateur station may make transmissions necessary to meet essential communication needs and facilitate relief actions.

(b) When a disaster disrupts normal communication systems in a particular area, the FCC may declare a temporary state of communication emergency. The declaration will set forth any special conditions and special rules to be observed by stations during the communication emergency. A request for a declaration of a temporary state of emergency should be directed to the EIC in the area concerned.

(c) A station in, or within 92.6 km of, Alaska may transmit emissions J3E and R3E on the channel at 5.1675 MHz for emergency communications. The channel must be shared with stations licensed in the Alaska-private fixed service. The transmitter power must not exceed 150 W.

§97.403 Safety of life and protection of property.

No provision of these rules prevents the use by an amateur station of any means of radiocommunication at its disposal to provide essential communication needs in connection with the immediate safety of human life and immediate protection of property when normal communication systems are not available.

§97.405 Station in distress.

(a) No provision of these rules prevents the use by an amateur station in distress of any means at its disposal to attract attention, make known its condition and location, and obtain assistance.

(b) No provision of these rules prevents the use by a station, in the exceptional circumstances described in paragraph (a), of any means of radiocommunications at its disposal to assist a station in distress.

§97.407 Radio amateur civil emergency service.

(a) No station may transmit in RACES unless it is an FCC-licensed primary, club, or military recreation station and it is certified by a civil defense organization as registered with that organization, or it is an FCC-licensed RACES station. No person may be the control operator of a RACES station, or may be the control operator of an amateur station transmitting in RACES unless that person holds a FCC-issued amateur operator license and is certified by a civil defense organization as enrolled in that organization.

(b) The frequency bands and segments and emissions authorized to the control operator are available to stations transmitting communications in RACES on a shared basis with the amateur service. In the event of an emergency which necessitates the invoking of the President's War Emergency Powers under the provisions of §706 of the Communications Act of 1934, as amended, 47 U.S.C. §606, RACES stations and amateur stations participating in RACES may only transmit on the following frequencies:

    (1) The 1800-1825 kHz, 1975-2000 kHz, 3.50-3.55 MHz, 3.93-3.98 MHz, 3.984-4.000 MHz, 7.079-7.125 MHz, 7.245-7.255 MHz, 10.10-10.15 MHz, 14.047-14.053 MHz, 14.22-14.23 MHz, 14.331-14.350 MHz, 21.047-21.053 MHz, 21.228-21.267 MHz, 28.55-28.75 MHz, 29.237-29.273 MHz, 29.45-29.65 MHz, 50.35-50.75 MHz, 52-54 MHz, 144.50-145.71 MHz, 146-148 MHz, 2390-2450 MHz segments;

(2) The 1.25 m, 70 cm and 23 cm bands; and

(3) The channels at 3.997 MHz and 53.30 MHz may be used in emergency areas when required to make initial contact with a military unit and for communications with military stations on matters requiring coordination.

(c) A RACES station may only communicate with:

(1) Another RACES station;

(2) An amateur station registered with a civil defense organization;

(3) A United States Government station authorized by the responsible agency to communicate with RACES stations;

(4) A station in a service regulated by the FCC whenever such communication is authorized by the FCC.

(d) An amateur station registered with a civil defense organization may only communicate with:

(1) A RACES station licensed to the civil defense organization with which the amateur station is registered;

(2) The following stations upon authorization of the responsible civil defense official for the organization with which the amateur station is registered:

(i) A RACES station licensed to another civil defense organization;

(ii) An amateur station registered with the same or another civil defense organization;

(iii) A United States Government station authorized by the responsible agency to communicate with RACES stations; and

(iv) A station in a service regulated by the FCC whenever such communication is authorized by the FCC.

(e) All communications transmitted in RACES must be specifically authorized by the civil defense organization for the area served. Only civil defense communications of the following types may be transmitted:

(1) Messages concerning impending or actual conditions jeopardizing the public safety, or affecting the national defense or security during periods of local, regional, or national civil emergencies;

(2) Messages directly concerning the immediate safety of life of individuals, the immediate protection of property, maintenance of law and order, alleviation of human suffering and need, and the combating of armed attack or sabotage;

(3) Messages directly concerning the accumulation and dissemination of public information or instructions to the civilian population essential to the activities of the civil defense organization or other authorized governmental or relief agencies; and

(4) Communications for RACES training drills and tests necessary to ensure the establishment and maintenance of orderly and efficient operation of the RACES as ordered by the responsible civil defense organizations served. Such drills and tests may not exceed a total time of 1 hour per week. With the approval of the chief officer for emergency planning in the applicable State, Commonwealth, District or territory, however, such tests and drills may be conducted for a period not to exceed 72 hours no more than twice in any calendar year.

Appendix 2

Countries that Share a Third Party Traffic Agreement with the United States:

Prefix	Country Name	Prefix	Country Name	Prefix	Country Name
V2	Antigua/Barbuda	C5	Gambia	ZP	Paraguay
LU	Argentina	9G	Ghana	OA	Peru
VK	Australia	J3	Grenada	DU	Philippines
V3	Belize	TG	Guatemala	VR6	Pitcairn Island*
CP	Bolivia	8R	Guyana	V4	St. Christopher/Nevis
T9	Bosnia-Herzegovina	HH	Haiti	J6	St. Lucia
PY	Brazil	HR	Honduras	J8	St. Vincent
VE	Canada	4X	Israel	9L	Sierra Leone
CE	Chile	6Y	Jamaica	ZS	South Africa
HK	Colombia	JY	Jordan	3DA	Swaziland
D6	Comoros	EL	Liberia	9Y	Trinidad/Tobago
TI	Costa Rica	V7	Marshall Islands	TA	Turkey
CO	Cuba	XE	Mexico	G	United Kingdom
HI	Dominican Republic	V6	Micronesia,	CX	Uruguay
J7	Dominica		Federated States of	YV	Venezuela
HC	Ecuador	YN	Nicaragua	4U1ITU - ITU,	Geneva
YS	El Salvador	HP	Panama	4U1VIC - VIC,	Vienna

*Since 1970, there has been an informal agreement between the United Kingdom and the US, permitting Pitcairn and US amateurs to exchange messages concerning medical emergencies, urgent need for equipment or supplies, and private or personal matters of island residents.

Note: US licensed amateurs may operate in the following US territories under their FCC license: The Northern Mariana Islands, Guam, Johnston Island, Midway Island, Kure Island, American Samoa, Wake Island, Wilkes Island, Peale Island, The Commonwealth of Puerto Rico and the US Virgin Islands.

Temporary Third Party Traffic Agreements

Note: During major disaster situations, administrations of countries may request temporary third party traffic agreements to facilitate the passage of emergency and health and welfare messages. W1AW bulletins carry announcements of temporary agreements.

Countries: _____

_____

_____

_____

Appendix 3

Common Power Connectors

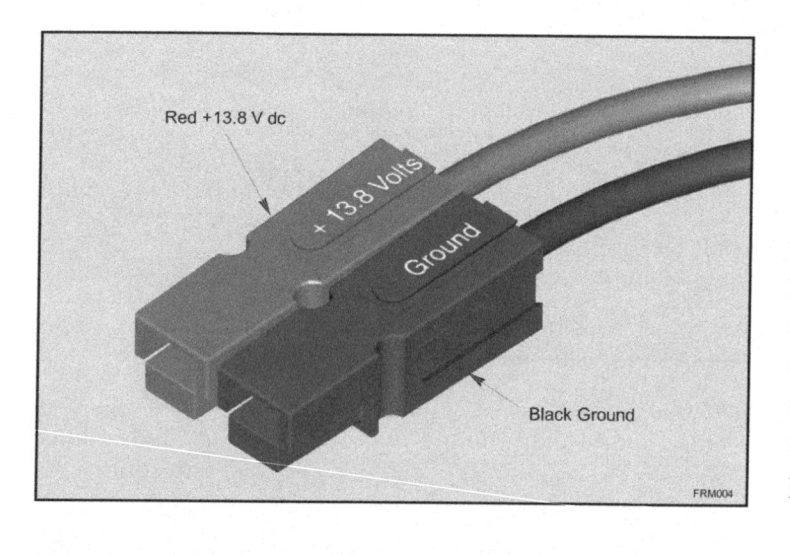

An increasing number of groups have adopted the 30 A Anderson Powerpole connector. Not only can the Powerpole handle greater current, it is also capable of being plugged and unplugged many hundreds of times (operations) without deterioration. These connectors are available from several sources, including Cable X-Perts (**www.cablexperts.com**) and PowerWerx (**www.powerwerx.com**). More information is available from the Anderson Power Products website at **www.andersonpower.com**. Look for these part numbers:

30 A	Complete Connector	Housing	Contact	Retaining Pin
Black	1330G4	1327G6	1331	110G16
Red	1330	1327	1331	110G16

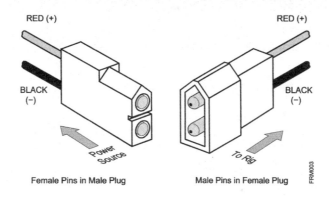

RED (+)   RED (+)

BLACK   BLACK
(–)   (–)

Power Source   To Rig

FRM003

Female Pins in Male Plug   Male Pins in Female Plug

The 12-A Molex 1545 series connector (part numbers: male, 03-09-2022; female, 03-09-1022) is adequate for low power mobile radios, handhelds and accessories.

It is important to find out which connector is being used in your area. Just to be sure, always check the voltage and polarity of a power source before you plug your equipment in, since polarity conventions are not always followed. Fusing the negative leads helps to protect equipment from ground-fault currents.

Appendix 4

Mutual Assistance Team (ARESMAT) Concept

The ARESMAT concept recognizes that a neighboring section's ARES resources can be quickly overwhelmed in a large-scale disaster. ARES members in the affected areas may be preoccupied with mitigation of their own personal situations and therefore not be able to respond in local ARES operations. Accordingly, communications support must come from ARES personnel outside the affected areas. This is when help may be requested from neighboring sections' ARESMAT teams. The following is a checklist of functions for ARESMAT leaders.

Pre-Departure Functions

- Notification of activation/assignment
- Credentials issued
- General and technical briefing
- Review host SEC's invitation
- Transportation
- Accommodations
- Expected length of deployment reviewed

In-Travel Functions

- Review situation status, and sitreps
- Review job assignments
- Checklists
- Affected area profile
- Mission disaster relief plan
- Maps
- Technical documents
- Contact lists
- Tactical operation procedures

Arrival Functions

- Check in with host ARES officials
- Obtain information:
    Frequencies in use
    Current actions
    Available personnel
    Communication and computer equipment
    Support facilities
    Host's ARES plan
- Establish initial intra-team communication net
- Establish HF or VHF channel back to the home
  section for morale traffic

In-situ Functions

- Initial assessment
- Monitor host ARES officials' communications
- Reduce duplication of effort
- Proper safety practices
- Daily critique of effectiveness

Pre-Demobilization and Demobilization Functions

- Extraction procedure negotiated
- Demobilization plan in effect
- Team critique begun

ARESMAT Member Qualifications

- High performance standards
- Qualifications
- Experience
- Team player
- Strong personal desire
- Strong interpersonal communication skills
- Emergency management knowledge
- Respected by officials and peers
- Available with consent of employer
- Physically fit

ARESMAT Concept Summary

It should be noted that there is a fine balance of authority over a deployed ARESMAT. The in-disaster SEC (or delegated authority) should be able to make decisions as to use and deployment of an incoming team. Therefore, an incoming team should be prepared to submit themselves to such authority; this is evidenced by the fact that any team, internal or external, has only a limited view of the overall operation. The supervising authorities will naturally have a better overview of the whole situation.

In turn, however, the in-disaster authority should be discouraged from abusing the resources of incoming teams. Should a team no longer be required, or a situation de-escalate, the team should be released at the earliest possible time, so that they may return home to their own lives.

The ARESMAT tool should be one of "last resort—better than nothing." Whenever possible, amateurs from the affected section should be used for support. It is a lot to ask of a volunteer to travel far from home, family and job for extended periods of arduous and potentially dangerous work.

Appendix 5
Understanding our Memoranda of Understanding

The premier justification for continued access to our piece of the spectrum pie is, and always will be, public service. A major part of our public service activity is conducted in the context of the ARRL's national-level formal agreements (MOUs) with "heavy hitters" of the emergency management community.

An MOU provides a framework for cooperation and coordination with agencies to which we as radio amateurs provide communication services. At the national level, this means periodic headquarters-to-headquarters contact to exchange news, views, information, and points of contact in the field. For example, ARRL staff attends the Annual Red Cross partnership meeting, along with representatives from other agencies and organizations that have MOUs with that organization. The idea is to get to know one another on a face-to-face basis, so that when an emergency happens, you know who to call and who you can count on.

At the local level, an MOU serves two purposes. First, it's a door opener. A new ARES group is more likely to be heard and taken seriously by a local National Weather Service (NWS) office when accompanied by the agreement document signed by the head of the agency. The served agency says, in effect, we have examined this organization of radio amateurs and have found them to be trustworthy and able to render substantial and needed services for our field operations in times of emergency.

Secondly, once your foot is in the door, the provisions of the MOU document spell out the capabilities and organization of the servers (us), the organization and needs of the served agency (them), and the methods of operation. These are broad guidelines that lead to the establishment of a local memorandum of understanding or similar document that sets forth the detailed operational plans and policies to be subscribed to by both parties during drills, and actual events.

The most important step here is to ensure that both parties to the local agreement have a realistic assessment of the resources brought to the table by the servers, and the needs of the served. Please contact your ARRL section leaders or ARRL Headquarters if you have questions about local or national-level MOUs. More information and the text of our various MOUs may be found online at **http://www.arrl.org/memoranda-of-understanding-mou**.

American Red Cross

ARRL and the Red Cross have had cooperative agreements since 1940. The current statement was signed in 2016. Chartered by Congress in 1905, the Red Cross provides relief to victims displaced by disaster, from the onset of disaster conditions to the recovery phase.

APCO International

The Association of Public-Safety Communications Officials (APCO) — International is made up of communications professionals in emergency medical, law enforcement, fire, search-and-rescue and other public safety fields.

Civil Air Patrol

Members of ARRL and the Civil Air Patrol (CAP) share common goals of serving the public through efficient and effective use of radio communications. To this end, members of both organizations engage in regular training to prepare for emergency and disaster communications. Members of both organizations provide important communications capability to the Homeland Security programs of the United States.

Department of Homeland Security—Citizen Corps

In June 2003, ARRL became an official affiliate program of Citizen Corps, an initiative within the

Department of Homeland Security to enhance public preparedness and safety. ARRL has worked closely with FEMA since 1984 when an MOU was signed that helped ARRL volunteers coordinate their services with emergency management at all levels of government. FEMA's job was as a "last responder," as opposed to first responders (the local, county and state emergency management agencies). Today, Citizen Corps groups are at the community level and state level to assist first responders.

National Association of Radio and Telecommunications Engineers

Founded in 1982, the National Association of Radio and Telecommunications Engineers (NARTE) offers an accredited certification program to qualified engineers and technicians, many of them amateur radio operators. Its other activities include participation as a commercial operator license examination manager. Its primary mission is to promote professional excellence within the telecommunications industry and related areas.

National Communications System

The National Communications System (NCS) is a confederation of 23 organizations across the Federal Government tasked with ensuring the availability of a viable national security and emergency preparedness telecommunications infrastructure.

National Weather Service

Amateur radio is almost synonymous with the SKYWARN program, the "eyes and ears" of the National Weather Service (NWS) during severe weather emergencies. Hams comprise the majority of SKYWARN volunteers, who report "ground truths" to local NWS offices, supplementing their sophisticated weather monitoring equipment.

Quarter Century Wireless Association

The Quarter Century Wireless Association (QCWA) and ARRL recognize each other's efforts to support, protect, promote and advance the Amateur Radio Service.

REACT International

ARRL and REACT (Radio Emergency Associated Communication Teams) share common goals in terms of emergency communication. The primary mission of REACT is "to provide public safety communications to individuals, organizations, and government agencies to save lives, prevent injuries, and give assistance wherever and whenever needed."

Salvation Army

The Salvation Army has provided services to victims of disasters for decades, and it's particularly active in the recovery stage of disasters. Along with many other agencies, the ARRL and the Salvation Army are member organizations to the National Voluntary Organizations Active in Disaster (NVOAD).

Society of Broadcast Engineers

ARRL is committed to helping develop future careers in RF Engineering and related technological fields. Our alliance with the Society of Broadcast Engineers (SBE) will help many hams gain the informational resources necessary to make sound career choices, as well as strengthen the exchange of technological innovation between hams and engineering professionals.

United States Power Squadrons

The United States Power Squadrons (USPS), a national boating and educational organization, is dedicated to making boating safer and more enjoyable. USPS formalized an MOU with ARRL in 2005 linking the two services in their efforts to better serve the public. USPS is a world leader in speaking out for and promoting the needs of all recreational boaters.

Appendix 6

Wilderness Protocol

The Wilderness protocol (see page 101, August 1995 *QST*) calls for hams in the wilderness to announce their presence on, and to monitor, the national calling frequencies for 5 minutes beginning at the top of the hour, every three hours, from 7 AM to 7 PM while in the back country. A ham in a remote location may be able to relay emergency information through another wilderness ham who has better access to a repeater. National calling frequencies are 52.525, 146.52, 223.50, 446.00, 1294.50 MHz.

ARES® Registration Form

Name: _____ Call Sign: _____ License Class _____

Address: _____ City: _____ State: _____ Zip: _____

Bus. phone: _____ Home phone: _____ Cell: _____

E-mail: _____ Check bands/modes you can operate:

Mode	HF	6 meters	2 meters	222 MHz	440 MHz	1.2 GHz
SSB						
CW						
FM						
Data						
Packet						
Mobile						

Can your home station be operated without commercial power?   Yes _____   No _____

If yes, what bands? _____

Signature: _____ Date:_____

Contact ARES and ARRL Section Leaders in your area: **www.arrl.org/sections**.

Incident Report Form

Please fill out this form and send a copy to your Emergency Coordinator and to ARRL Headquarters. When reporting to ARRL Headquarters, you can use the online reporting form (FSD-157): **http://www.arrl.org/fsd-157-public-service-activity-report**.

Nature of emergency/disaster: _____

_____

Dates of activity: _____   Places or areas involved: _____

Nets and/or frequencies used: _____

Number of participating amateurs: _____   Number of messages handled: _____

Agencies supported: _____

ARES leadership officials managing deployment: _____

Your name/call: _____ Signature: _____ Date: _____

E-Mail address: _____

 # Incident Log Sheet

Date/Time	Event	Msg No.	Message From	Message To	Assigned Net Frequency	Assigned By

Incident Log Sheet

Date/Time	Event	Msg No.	Message From	Message To	Assigned Net Frequency	Assigned By

Appendix 7
ARRL Emergency Courses

EC-001—Introduction to Emergency Communications. This course is designed to provide basic knowledge and tools for any emergency communications volunteer. The course has six sections with 28 lesson topics, and includes a selection of student activities, knowledge review quizzes, and a final assessment. The course is conducted entirely online and can be completed at your own pace, allowing you to work according to your own schedule. You must pace yourself to complete all the required material in the allotted time. For further information and to register for the course, visit **www.arrl.org/online-course-catalog**.

EC-016—Public Service and Emergency Communications Management for Radio Amateurs. This course is designed to train licensed amateur radio operators who will be in leadership and managerial roles, organizing other volunteers to support public service activities and communications emergencies. In this course, you will learn how radio amateurs prepare and organize to support local community events, and, working in coordination with governmental and other emergency response organizations, deploy their services to provide communications when needed in an emergency. For further information and to register for the course, visit **www.arrl.org/online-course-catalog**.

Notes

Notes